D1175739

cabinosity

Pull your family together before
your things pull them apart.

cabinosity

Pull your family together before
your things pull them apart.

Peter McClellan and Kelly Schackman

<u>**DISCLAIMER OF LEGAL ADVICE AND ALL WARRANTIES.**</u> THE INFORMATION CONTAINED IN THIS BOOK IS NOT LEGAL ADVICE AND SHOULD NOT BE RELIED UPON TO REPLACE THE COUNSEL OF QUALIFIED PROFESSIONALS, INCLUDING BUT NOT LIMITED TO ATTORNEY(S) AND FINANCIAL PLANNER(S). PLEASE CHECK WITH YOUR CHOSEN PROFESSIONAL(S) BEFORE PROCEEDING WITH ANY ESTATE PLANNING OR SETTLEMENT.

INFORMATION IN THIS BOOK IS NOT GUARANTEED TO BE CORRECT, COMPLETE OR UP-TO-DATE. THE LAW CHANGES RAPIDLY, DIFFERS FROM JURISDICTION TO JURISDICTION, AND IS ALSO SUBJECT TO VARYING INTERPRETATIONS BY DIFFERENT COURTS, GOVERNMENT AND ADMINISTRATIVE BODIES. 401(K) LATTE COMPANY AND THE REEL LEGACY CONVERSATION COMPANY, LLC. (THE "COMPANIES") DO NOT GUARANTEE ANY INFORMATION CONTAINED IN THIS BOOK TO BE ACCURATE TO CURRENT LAW.

THE INFORMATION IN THIS BOOK DOES NOT CREATE ANY WARRANTIES. THE COMPANIES DISCLAIM ANY AND ALL WARRANTIES TO THE FULLEST EXTENT ALLOWABLE BY LAW, WHETHER ANY WARRANTY IS ORAL OR WRITTEN, EXPRESS OR IMPLIED.

THE COMPANIES ARE NOT RESPONSIBLE FOR ANY LOSS, INJURY, CLAIM, LIABILITY, OR DAMAGE RELATED TO USE OF THE INFORMATION CONTAINED IN THIS BOOK.

The reader is strongly encouraged to think seriously about their own legacy and how to positively influence future generations.

ISBN 978-0-615-20119-1

cabinosity defined

ca • bin • os • i • ty   (kā-*bĭn*-**os**-i-tee)

n.

1. The animosity between family members that can occur due to an inherited cabin.

contents

introduction

Not many things sadden me more than witnessing seemingly close families fractured over the estate settlement. The damage to sibling relationships is irreparable in many cases. I've seen it in clients' families in my years as a financial advisor, and to a very limited extent, I've been a part of some of the unpleasant rifts at the passing of my own parents. My siblings and I got through the process of settling our parents' estate "relatively" unscathed, but there were some things that were done and said that still linger. More than a decade has flown by, and to this day, there are some challenges between my siblings that would trouble my parents if they were alive today. To my brother's and sisters' credit, we have maintained our relationships with each other over the years, honoring our beloved parents. We are still a family and care about each other. Unfortunately, many families who settle their parents' estate can't say the same.

People today seem fixated on "fairness" and entitlement as if they were children splitting the last cookie in the package. Everyone has their perspective on what is "fair" and what they have a "right" to rather than what is right. As a financial advisor, I have had retirees convince me that their children would never fight, and I naively believed them. However, those kids who would never fight seem to do so over the most absurd things. While we desperately need to get our legal estate plan established or updated, (Sadly many a person still die in this country without ever getting even a will written!) we need to go far beyond the legal aspects of our plan to the relational aspects. It is imperative that we initiate honest, open conversations with our heirs about the spirit and the heart that we will want them to bring to the settlement table. The fact is we are all going to die, and yet, we pretend it will never arrive. It will, in fact, arrive and estates large, small and everything in between will need to be settled.

Guarding our words is difficult especially after the death of a loved one. Things are often said in the heat of the moment—cutting deeply. Benjamin Franklin was quoted as saying: "Remember not only to say the right thing in the right place, but far more difficult still, to leave unsaid the wrong thing at the tempting moment." Words are not easily forgotten or forgiven. So many people go to their graves hating the sibling who spoke harshly or clamored for their "rights" before thinking. Resentments build particularly deep for the passive one that took the non-combative path saying, "You take it all. I'm not going to fight you for any of it." Years later they become incensed that their sibling, in fact, did take it all. The resulting wounds are often too deep, too painful and too scarring.

We need to verbalize what we want to happen at our deaths. We can't possibly think of every item we own and direct it toward a beneficiary; though, we certainly do the best we can. To the point, however, we can talk to our children about honor and respect and how happy we'd be if they would come to the settlement table with the right spirit—a generous spirit focused on blessing others rather than clawing to get a "fair" share.

I am a Baby Boomer and can attest to the fact that far too many of us are self-absorbed. We have only known very good economic times, twisting our perspective on life. If there has ever been a generation that could gain from the common sense, wisdom and loving instruction from its parents, it's this generation. We all need to be reminded of what really matters in life, and we need someone who loves us enough to courageously instruct us in honor and right living.

If those in their twilight years will show this type of leadership, not only will they diminish the looming division and disunity that threatens their family, but they will also bless future generations with a firm legacy on which to stand. Sadly, far too many retirees will shirk this responsibility with a mealy-mouthed response like, "Well, the kids are raising kids of their own. I don't want to meddle." You're not meddling when it comes to communicating your wishes to your heirs about your possessions. You're especially not meddling if you turn them back to the basics: love of family, love of country and love of God. Don't fall into the soup with them. They need you to lead.

Admittedly, most of the following short stories camp on the dark side. They are a collection of actual situations I have witnessed both personally and as a financial advisor with clients over the years. Each story is followed by **the goal of this book is to get families talking** questions and tips meant to get you thinking about how your own estate is designed, how it will transfer to your heirs and how to pursue unity for your family. The goal of this book is to get families talking. Break the "no talk" rule about an uncomfortable topic: death and what happens when you're gone. I'm not so naive to think these stories would end family conflicts. Some conflicts may actually occur. Good! I hope they do, especially if conflicts lead to peaceful resolutions and greater character development. I hope some of the harder work can get done now so that your heirs won't have to deal with them when you are gone. That would be wonderful. Or as my late father, John F. McClellan from Jersey City would say, "Oh that would be beautiful! Beautiful!" He was a great guy! I miss him. It will forever pain me that my children didn't have the chance to know him.

something so right

As told from the perspective of Peter McClellan.

I want to start off this little book of stories with a wonderfully positive story that impacted our family many years ago. Every family has its own story to tell. Every family has its share of "nuts and fruits." The McClellans are no different. However, here's one story I'm proud to share because it was good—very good—and well worth remembering.

It was a cold, snowy night in the '30's in Jersey City, New Jersey. The times were hard and my grandfather, who had worked late, was about to leave to walk home. My grandmother, concerned about him walking home in the weather, called for a taxi rather than have her oldest son (my dad), John, accompany his father home, as was their custom. Tragically, as the taxi neared the shipyards, it was caught between the old iron gates that came down to protect people from oncoming trains. Sure enough, a train was fast approaching. The taxi driver, knowing his vehicle, was able to open his door quickly and exit the vehicle while my grandfather fumbled around in the dark looking for an unfamiliar door handle in the back seat. It was too late. The train demolished the vehicle and took my grandfather's life with it. My grandmother, who at the time was only in her 40's, died shortly thereafter. We are all convinced it was of a broken heart and a sense of guilt because she had sent for the very taxi in which her husband died.

I am certain that the deep sense of legacy that has been imprinted on me was derived from the following events. My Aunt Helen, the oldest of ten children, bought a house in the suburbs with her husband, my Uncle John Joe, and took in her eight siblings—several of which were only grade-schoolers. My father was one of the older kids, but he still enjoyed seeing his family stay together. Their family pulled together through some of the worst years our country has known, and yet, those years were some of the best of their lives. My dad and the older kids worked to pay bills and do their part. While they all mourned the loss of their parents, they pulled together and not only survived, but also grew closer as a family.

My Aunt Helen and Uncle John Joe, though starting a family of their own, understood the value of family and placed it as a top priority in their lives. They honored their parents by making it their mission to see that their siblings were taken care of and that the family stayed together. This, of course, came to

they understood the value of family and placed it as top priority

them at significant personal sacrifice of time, energy and money. As I reflect on what it meant in terms of selfless sacrifice, my Aunt Helen and Uncle John Joe were nothing short of heroes. I don't have the details of exactly how it all transpired, but what they accomplished was truly remarkable. What an amazing legacy and model of the parent-honoring spirit we all should possess at the passing of our parents.

I don't know much about my uncle's roots, but I am convinced that my Aunt Helen was greatly impacted by her mother (my grandmother). I've been told my grandmother cherished her own family more than anything else on the planet. She was a Russian Jew who had immigrated to Brooklyn, New York before the turn of the last century. By marrying my grandfather, whose family roots went back to Ireland, she'd married outside of her faith and crossed the line. Her family had a funeral for her; she was disowned. Her sisters would sneak away from Brooklyn to Jersey City occasionally to see her, but she had effectively lost her parents and the sense of belonging to a family.

I never met her or my grandfather, but my dad spoke of them like they were from another world. He loved them and respected them long after they were gone. His brothers and sisters all felt the same. As I reflect back on these events, I'm convinced my grandmother had been restored to family life by the man she loved and the children that loved her so deeply. My Aunt Helen and her siblings didn't inherit much material wealth from my grandparents, but they did inherit values from them that are more precious than gold.

wake up and smell the coffee questions

☕ If your children (or grandchildren) are still minors, have you (or your children) made certain that they will be adequately taken care of if something should happen to you? For example: have you carefully chosen a guardian and are you properly insured?

☕ Do you think your children will remain close when you die? Why or why not?

☕ Do they understand what serving each other really means?

☕ Is there anything you could do now to help ensure they will be unified when you are gone?

☕ If your children are adults, do you have a trusted relative or friend that could serve as a "stand-in" parent?

☕ Are your children familiar with your family roots?

☕ Do they know some important family stories that they could share with their children?

peter's legacy building tips

»   Call a family meeting or conference call and speak to your children about how you would like to see them get along when you are gone. Make sure you are in charge of the meeting.

»   Choose a trusted friend or relative that could be available if your children would need some parental advice when you're gone. Make them aware of how important it is for your children to get along.

»   Provide opportunities for your children to serve you and each other.

»   Have a family album made for each child that commemorates the wonderful family memories.

»   Document the family tree and family stories.

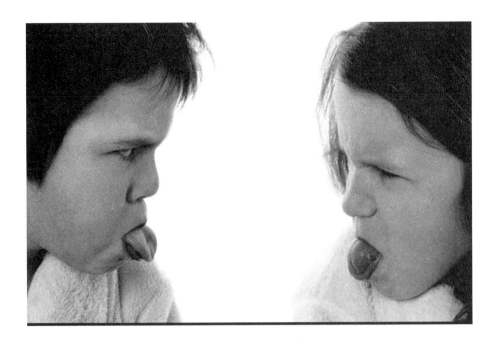

cabinosity

The Minnesota Brainerd Lakes area is truly magical in the summer. Families spend years of summers at "the cabin," building memories that span generations. But what happens when not everyone in the family cherishes the beloved cabin? The following short story explores one family's struggle with what to do with Mom and Dad's cabin.

Ray and Alice were fifteen when they met and fell in love at the roller rink in their rural farming community. Nine days after their 52nd wedding anniversary, Alice buried her beloved Ray. They weathered the typical highs and lows of a life spent together. They raised three boys into three fine men. All three boys followed their father's examples of a strong work ethic and of responsibly providing for their families. They married women who kept short accounts of their wrong doings and complemented their strengths.

The boys captured their mother's zeal for others and her zest for life. She had a flair for the dramatic, and her sons resorted to the same antics at some of the most inopportune times. True to her devotion and love for her life's mate, Alice slipped quietly and unexpectedly into eternity exactly one week after she laid Ray to rest.

The boys and their wives met shortly after burying both parents. They gathered in the small but tidy house that had been their parents' homestead for all their married life. The shock and grief were palpable. In no time they drew comfort from the familiar surroundings of their youth. Their tears were often interrupted by side-splitting laughter as they regaled each other with stories of their parents' idiosyncrasies. They cajoled and complained about Mom and Dad's approach to life when they were raising their brood, and even more so, as they navigated the aging process— which wasn't always graceful.

They quickly and easily divided the meager possessions. For the boys, meaningful memorabilia from time spent with Dad in days long gone, a bauble or two for the ladies and a small remembrance for each of the seven grandchildren. The family cabin was last on the agenda for the day. Ray's parents had built the rustic two-room shanty when Ray was a small boy. To call it a cabin was a stretch. But the cabin was intricately woven into the boy's tapestry of their formative years. As their teen years encroached upon tradition, trips to the cabin were replaced by cars and girls and more noble pursuits than a trophy walleye. That is, except for Tom, the middle son. He continued to make the four-hour excursion up north as often as possible. When he had his own kids, the cabin became an integral part of his family's legacy. He even tried to talk his wife into having their babies baptized in the lake instead of the fount of their local church.

Tom felt like someone deflated his lungs when John, the oldest, proposed they get a real estate appraisal on the property, sell it and divide the profit three ways. When Tom found his voice it was barley audible, "Dad's pop built that cabin. Some of our best summer memories are there. Dad has not been in the ground ten days and you would dishonor him this way for a few measly bucks?"

Before John could recover from the barrage leveled by his closest brother, Tom continued with even greater fervor, "I have spent every Memorial Day weekend up there cleaning and repairing the place for the summer and again Labor Day weekends to winterize it. I invested my own time and money when things desperately needed updating. Your Cindy sure didn't complain when I installed the indoor plumbing. When Mom and Dad were struggling with money thanks to Dad's health, I paid the property taxes. My kids love the cabin like I did. How can you even think of selling it?"

John defiantly straightened up in his chair, "Scott and I haven't been to the cabin since high school except for the few occasions Mom planned get-togethers. Cindy hates being there—the bugs, the musty couch—entertaining the girls with only a lake, a couple of loons and no TV. It's not a pleasant adventure for us, Tom. Scott told me he feels the same way. I think selling is the most equitable way to resolve this."

Tom drew a deep anguished breath, "If you force your way and sell our cabin, this will be my last family event ever. We've buried our parents, and I will have nothing further to do with either one of you. I will be forced to consider that you reside in the same cemetery as Mom and Dad."

> if you force your way and sell our cabin this will be my last family event ever

19

A couple of years have gone by since those words were exchanged. Unfortunately, there has been no resolution. Even though the cabin hasn't been sold, the boys don't speak much except for Scott's and John's constant complaints to each other about missing out on part of their inheritance because Tom continues to go fishing as if nothing is wrong. Tom avoids his brothers, fearing they'll push the sale of the property. Scott and John would just like their share of the inheritance but are annoyed that there has been no offer on Tom's part to buy them out.

Before Ray and Alice passed on, the boys had always enjoyed each others company. Ray and Alice would never have dreamed that things would turn so sour. Neither did the boys. But that's how it is, and it's not likely to change anytime soon. How could the very cabin that housed so many precious family memories be the source of resentments that keep brothers divided? You can bet this was never in their great grandfather's mind as he dug the footings and put the place together.

wake up and smell the coffee questions

☕ Can the interested parties afford to buy out the other less interested family members? If they can't afford to buy them out, can you afford to make it fair in the way you leave the balance of your estate?

☕ Do you have a child who erroneously feels "entitled" to the property because he/she is the oldest or loves it the most? Whatever the reason, an entitlement mindset will almost always lead to conflict. Have you confronted and challenged that child's thinking? Is he/she willing to change to make things right? Are you as big a part of the problem as the child? Everyone better grow up quickly and get this conversation moving before it is too late.

☕ Is there a child who not only contributed time and energy into the cabin's upkeep, but contributed financially? Have you kept track of the dollars contributed by that child? Should those legitimate contributions be taken into account as you plan a fair distribution of your estate?

☕ Do your children fully understand the "work" involved in keeping and maintaining the cabin? Are they prepared to plan and schedule not only the future use of the cabin, but also the maintenance and repairs?

☕ Is it realistic to expect that your family will use the cabin forever? If not, what should determine its sale?

peter's legacy building tips

» Perhaps the thought of your children fighting over the place that fostered some of your most treasured memories is over the top—too unpleasant to even ponder. Start pondering.

» Initiate the conversation with your children: "What happens to the cabin when I'm gone?" Insist on the conversation even if it is met with resistance.

» It's your cabin. What right do your children have to fight over it while you are alive? ANSWER: they have no right. Unless it burns down, the cabin isn't going away. While I am not suggesting arson, not resolving the situation before you die is worse than it burning down. Don't leave resentments and childish behavior under the surface until after you die. Get them out in the open now. Be "the bad guy" if necessary. It's okay if they get mad at you.

» You've weighed all sides. Now make a decision as to what you want to have happen with your cabin when you die. Present your decision to your children. Ask them to honor your decision now and after your death.

» As the leader of your family, if you have decided the risks of disunity are too great, then do what is best for your family.

» If you decide that your children will benefit from keeping the cabin, work out scheduling its use and maintenance. Have a fund available to pay for upkeep. Determine who will be managing all of this. Give them guidelines for an eventual exit strategy if one or more of your children doesn't want the cabin any longer.

» Lead your family. Show them that you value them more than a material possession. The cabin, like a house, is never what makes a home. It's the people.

the snow birds that never flew south

A loving son recalls the pain in seeing his parents' retirement whittled away by a sibling. If only his folks' savings could've hit the road in an RV.

"WE'RE SPENDING OUR CHILDREN'S INHERITANCE." That bumper sticker proudly displayed on the back of a big ole' RV always made me chuckle.

I wish my parents had spent our inheritance when they had the chance. I wish they had lolled away their winters basking in the warm Florida sun—eating freshly caught fish for supper—my dad all decked out in his white patent leather loafers and matching belt to hold up his plaid polyester slacks. I wish they had hours of vacation films we could view together. I wish they had traveled the country to visit our scattered family in a big ole' RV with the bumper sticker "WE'RE SPENDING OUR CHILDREN'S INHERITANCE" plastered across the bumper. Sadly, this was not my parents' legacy.

Our little Midwestern family was nothing spectacular. It consisted of my folks, my sister Kate, brothers David, Will and Jeff and myself. Dad drove truck for the local dairy, and Mom stayed home and raised the kids. They had a strong work ethic, believed in saving a little and loving us big.

They say every family has its black sheep, and ours was no exception. I am always curious what makes just one kid go awry in a family whose history is otherwise uneventful. Jeff was our black sheep. He started with petty juvenile pranks in his teens and graduated to a criminal path likely to drive him to an untimely death.

every family has its black sheep, and we were no exception

My parents didn't get to spend their hard earned savings in retirement or leave a little nest egg to us because Jeff's antics slowly bled them dry. There was bail money, the lawyers' fees and court costs—an attempt to give him one more chance. He surely would be responsible after this lesson was learned, they felt. Then he would need help with rent or a new car after he had demolished vehicle after vehicle.

We staged several family meetings to try and talk some sense into my parents, to no avail. Their rescuing Jeff had long ceased being a help; instead, only a hindrance to him taking responsibility for his life and his choices. During one particularly long and cold Minnesota winter, we tried to encourage my folks to take just a short trip to Florida. My mother wouldn't hear of it, "What if something happens to Jeff? He could need us, and we could be loafing out on the beach somewhere. What if they found him face down in a snow bank?"

The call came late into the night. I couldn't understand my mother's words at first through her hysterical sobs. The tragic death visited upon our family was not Jeff's; my father had died from a sudden heart attack.

There never was a winter trip to Florida. There was barely enough money left to support my mom's basic needs. We did bury Dad in white patent leather loafers with a matching white belt (sort of Florida style) to try and make us feel a little lighter in our hearts.

Now whenever I see that big ole' RV with the bumper sticker on the back I no longer chuckle; it's a bittersweet reminder of what could have been.

wake up and smell the coffee questions

- Do you have a child who gets lots of extra time, attention or money as compared to your other children?

- How do your other children feel about it? Do they have legitimate concerns for your well-being in retirement, or are their concerns unjustified?

- "I guess I'd better not die." Unhealthy dynamics only tend to worsen after parents are gone. Are you deceiving yourself into thinking it will all work out when you are gone? You are probably in denial.

- Do you expect that your other children will provide the type of "care" that you are providing to that one child? Should they? Is that the right thing to expect?

- Is there something you should do that should have been done a long time ago?

peter's legacy building tips

» Maybe the extra time, attention and money flowing towards that one child is legitimate. Perhaps you need to confront selfishness in the other children. It all hinges on legitimacy. Talk it up.

» Maybe the high maintenance adult child desperately needs to grow up and face reality. Are you as much of the problem as he/she is? Show tough love now. The longer you wait the more difficult the situation will be. Your family will respect you if you make decisions that demonstrate your willingness to lead.

» Seek the wise counsel of your pastor, rabbi, priest or trusted friend whose opinion you respect. These types of issues may or may not be black and white. Others who care about you and your family may offer some much needed insight. Seek them out. At a minimum you could use their prayers and emotional support.

» If you come to the conclusion that the appropriate response is "tough love," ask someone to hold you accountable to follow through as you learn to stop enabling that difficult child.

» Once you have stopped enabling bad behavior, you and the rest of the family would benefit from forgiving the wrongs that you suffered. This doesn't mean a return to enabling, it means you lead your family by harboring no resentments. Forgive him/her. You all will continue to suffer if you don't.

step-mommy dearest

A son shares how he helplessly watched his father's second wife be awarded his dad's estate, lock, stock and barrel.

Grandma used to say, "Blood runs thicker than water, but greed goes deeper than blood." OK, I know my stepmother's not blood, but I thought 25 years of marriage should count for something. My grandmother's sage opinion rang through my head as the judge's gavel brought me crashing back to reality.

> blood runs thicker than water, but greed runs deeper than blood

"Mr. Hayward, I have reached my ruling in your case against your stepmother, Mrs. John Hayward," the judge stated clearly. "You have the legal right to view your father's last will and testament. In regards to any further action, however, I strongly suggest you do not pursue this matter further. Your father's will is iron clad, and it will waste your resources as well as the court's time. I suggest you try to reach an amicable solution amongst yourselves. This case is concluded."

I slowly rose to my feet willing myself not to look in the direction of my stepmother's smug face. She said there was nothing in the will that pertained to me, and now I would have the chance to see for myself.

My mom and dad divorced when I was eleven. Soon after, he married Penny. Contrary to popular custom, my three sisters and I went to live with Dad, our new Mom and four new sisters. I didn't have much about life figured out, but I'll tell you one thing for certain—the Brady Bunch was a big fat lie.

It didn't take long to figure out the pecking order in our new household. Penny's girls ruled the roost and got my dad's full attention and resources. It wasn't that my dad didn't love us, but Penny was a force to be reckoned with if she didn't get her way. You know the adage "If Mama ain't happy, ain't nobody happy." My dad was determined not to fail in this marriage, no matter what the cost.

My sisters took the favoritism in stride and managed to grow up with healthy relationship skills and few scars. I, on the other hand, could not reconcile the injustice of it all. I couldn't earn Dad's notice by positive means, but boy did he pay attention when I started calling from the police station. His wallet wouldn't open wide enough for new football cleats, but the cash flowed to pay bail and lawyers' fees. I think as he aged he realized the role his disloyalty in my youth played out in my bad behavior later.

A strange emptiness enveloped me when I received the news of my father's death. I had always wished for Penny to go first so I could recapture my father's affection. Now, the only thing that remained of my dad was any meager possessions he might have left me. Penny made it very clear when she called to let me know of my dad's passing there would be no money forthcoming. I had sucked that well dry through my wrangling with the law.

I had hoped to inherit his old Chevy pickup. It wasn't worth much to anyone, but it bore 'Hayward and Sons' on its rusty side panels, and I was the only Hayward son. The pickup reminded me of a happier time when Dad was really Dad.

Penny and I met in the judge's chambers as I looked over the legal proclamation without meeting her eyes. There was indeed no monetary provision for me or my sisters. All that was his went to her and, if she departed first, all that was hers belonged to him.

Later that week, I was running errands when I spotted the old Chevy. There wasn't a Hayward son behind the wheel. Proudly sitting in the driver's seat was my stepsister's husband. I don't believe my dad intended the hurt he caused in my youth, and I don't imagine he thought my stepmother would leave us completely out of her inheritance. I am certain he meant to see to her needs believing she would share the wealth. Intentional or not, his betrayal had unfortunately come full circle.

wake up and smell the coffee questions

- Are you in a second marriage? Do you have children from a previous marriage? Do you have a prenuptial agreement in place that protects your children's interests or at least helps you to remember them when your things "settle"?

- While you can't undo the past, is there some way you can tell your children from your first marriage that they are important to you? If they aren't important to you now, will you consider building a bridge to them with the intention of setting things right?

- Is your "Penny" truly a jerk that needs to be confronted? Is this person your spouse? If so, do not pass GO. Get to a marriage counselor right away!

peter's legacy building tips

» Don't expect an immediate open door on the part of your estranged children. Maybe if you move slowly and consistently, you could win them over in time and build a bridge of friendship. It is worth trying. We have all made mistakes in life and have unintentionally hurt others. While we are still living, we have an opportunity to do what is right. It's never too late to do the right thing. Okay, so you've never been a bridge builder. Today is a fine day to start.

» You are the spouse of the parent who has emotionally "abandoned" the children of a previous marriage. Be the peacemaker and encourage your spouse to open up contact with those children before it is too late.

5

not so special plate

This next story illustrates how important it is to invest in even the tough or uncomfortable conversations sooner rather than later. As told by Katherine, one of the three devoted daughters.

"Mom, I can't talk to you about this stuff let alone even think about you dying. You aren't ever going to be gone, so please let's change the subject." I pleaded like I was twelve again.

My mother tried to defuse the tears that were ready to spill out of my eyes. She gently cajoled, "Katherine, I know I don't have much, but I listen to my friends' stories, and I don't want my daughters torn apart like their families over what little junk I leave behind."

"Mom," I protested a little too loudly for the quaint coffee shop Mom invited me to for this chat, "Julia, Laura and I have been best friends more than we have ever been sisters. We shared Barbies when we were little girls. We shared recipes and child rearing successes and failures when we were starting young families. Now we swap tips on hiding crow's feet or what a hero a girdle can be for a high school class reunion. We love each other, Mom, and we respect you too much to let possessions come between us. It's not like the Hope Diamond is hidden in your underwear drawer!" Being the oldest, very strong willed, and determined, I could intimidate my mother. So we moved on to less volatile topics like the blight that was destroying my prized pot of impatiens and gossip from the last meeting of the Red Hat Society.

I often look back on that morning and wonder if she knew she would only be with us five more months. We could visit her dismal need to discuss the dispersal of all her earthly belongings later. I thought I had more time, a lot more time.

Now all I had on my hands was time. Time to ponder and reflect and come up with no good answer as to why a simple hand-painted plate was the nemesis for the three year estrangement from my two beloved sisters, my greatest friends on Earth.

now all I had on my hands was time

We left the cemetery arm in arm, tears flowing freely as only girls do. We took refuge at Mom's little apartment. We sipped heartily from her chipped and mismatched cups. The strong coffee helped to nip the chill we all felt despite the early warm spring day. Her funeral had been lovely, filled with lots of friends. She would have been so pleased. Her apartment didn't feel like home to us. She had moved there after we were all married. We did feel comforted sitting amidst the things she loved and had brought her a small measure of joy. We knew the task at hand—what to do with Mom's stuff—would not be made easier by delaying the process. We moved into mechanical mode with little fanfare.

Her clothes were easy; we bagged them up neatly for Goodwill. No one suggested we would be any more fashionable in our late seventies. The pictures took longer causing many twists and turns down memory lane. We took the snapshots of our own families and evenly divided the neutral shots—done. Fate smiled on us with her jewelry. There were three rings, one each having its sentimental tug at our heart strings. There was a bevy of cheap gaudy costume jewelry. Baubles she would pick up at the Five and Dime or garage sales. We divided this stash into three large piles—a treasure trove for our little granddaughters. Mom's kitchen was simple. A microwave, a few dishes and several old cook books. We all lived in much bigger houses decked out with all the latest in cooking utensils to host the family gatherings. Mom didn't require much.

Then we happened upon the plate. It was a simple red plate with little splashes of white paint, which as children we saw as daisies. In the center painted in a lazy scroll was the phrase, "You Are Special." We couldn't remember a time when the plate wasn't a part of our family. It was initially brought out to honor the birthday girl. Then we extended its purpose as we grew. We used it to praise a well earned report card, a place on the softball team, surviving eighth grade biology without throwing up on the dissected frog. We used the plate to cheer someone up when they had a particularly difficult day or a bad break-up. When we started having our babies, two sisters would bring the plate to the hospital laden with chocolate dipped strawberries to rejoice in God's newest gift to our family.

One plate, three sisters who now live miles apart in far away cities.

Julia suggested a time-share-type arrangement, "We could each keep the plate four months out of the year."

Laura, forever the pragmatist, shot holes through Julia's proposal, "What if it broke during shipping? The odds are pretty great mailing it all over the country. And more disturbing, what if one of us has a "You Are Special" moment when we aren't in possession of the plate?"

We hashed out several other scenarios, all to no avail. I like to think it was our grief and not our selfishness and greed that came to bear. We each began to lay out our best Perry Mason argument of why we should be the sole proprietor of the plate. I was the oldest and had more years with the plate, more memories. Julia felt she had invested more time with Mom in her twilight years; she had lived the closest. Laura was the baby and she felt cheated. She should be the rightful owner because she had the fewest years to feel special.

> I like to think it was our grief and not our selfishness and greed that came to bear

The specific details are foggy now; too many tears to even see history accurately. We were tugging on the plate with the vengeance of a group of two-year olds. It seemed like a slow motion replay as the plate suddenly flew into the air and shattered on Mom's yellowed linoleum floor.

Three years passed and we managed to maintain our relationship, but there has been a cooling of our warm, spontaneous friendship. We are still grieving the loss of our mother; she was a centering influence that pulled us together. That force is gone, and we are busy leading our own lives and families. The destruction of that special plate is still a cause for lamentation.

Odd that something as monetarily insignificant as a plate could be a source of pain and discomfort. I regret not letting Mom talk a bit more about what was on her mind regarding her few meager possessions. She was on to something. I wish I would have let her tell me the horror stories of how things went so wrong with her friends' families. I think she'd be proud of us for mending things, but she'd be saddened to know we experienced the very thing she feared might happen. How on earth did she know?

wake up and smell the coffee questions

☕ Have you let your kids shut you down when you bring up issues surrounding your passing?

☕ If you haven't broached this end-of-life topic, what is preventing you from doing so? Are you afraid? If so, of what?

☕ What is gnawing at you that you have not aired with your children out of fear of upsetting them?

☕ It may not be a plate for you, but is there a material item that represents rich traditions and pleasant family memories?

☕ Do you have a list of your material possessions that you want to go to your children?

peter's legacy building tips

» The longer the topic is taboo, the bigger the emotional hurdles will be when the conversations present themselves after your funeral. The more you leave to post-mortem settling, the higher the risk of nasty conflicts. You won't be there to speak truth and help them through it.

» If you have identified things you need to communicate or if there are items the kids could fight over, why not talk them through it? Schedule a family meeting.

» Have the kids list five items that they might wish to have after you are gone. You may begin to see some potential for conflict.

» Don't let them shut you down. Show leadership. If it erupts into unpleasant conflict between the children, be thankful you are there to help resolve it. Be the "bad" guy if the situation calls for it. It is never too late to lead, speak truth, and challenge a wrong attitude in your children.

» Maybe you are a person who avoids conflict at any costs. Count the cost of avoiding this one: permanent family disunity, hatred and resentment. Step out of your comfort zone this time. Regardless of how your children treat each other when you are gone, at least they will know, "What would Mom or Dad do?" At least you will be remembered as a peacemaker. That spirit is contagious and may actually be part of your legacy. It may be part of what they bring to the conflict resolution table in the future.

PLATE SUGGESTION:

Knowing that darn plate will be problematic, here's a thought. Why not take a very nice photograph of the plate and have it beautifully framed for each of your children? The actual plate goes into the casket when you're gone. Okay, you may not like that idea, but at least it's a way to start the resolution ball rolling. Maybe the three year (or potentially lifetime) cooling off of the girls' friendship could have been avoided.

the wedding ring gimmie gimmie

An only-daughter recounts the passing of her mother, a fight for a ring, loss of a relationship and the desire for just one do-over.

Life's twists and turns don't always take us down the path we would like. Aren't there times in our lives when we would like to be able to write our own script or at least have some editing options? I always thought it would have been a good idea if God had given us do-over punch cards. Not an unlimited amount of punches mind you, just a precious few—and no wasted punches on decisions like bad prom dates. No, you would have to carefully choose the situations you would like to do over. I've had several occasions that, in hindsight, I would love the chance to do differently. Let me be indulgent, and tell you about one such time.

I was the only girl in a two sibling family. My father died at an early age, and Mom and I forged a special bond. We had the usual mother daughter ups and downs, but always shared a mutual love and respect for one another. In my mid-twenties, love carried me far across America to marry a career military man. As we moved from base to base I maintained as close a relationship with my mom as Ma-Bell and the occasional flight home allowed me.

My brother, Chuck, married a lovely woman named Carol. They remained in our home town and the load of seeing to our mother's needs fell in the capable and willing hands of Carol. As my mother aged and her needs intensified she moved into a small room in Chuck and Carol's modest home. My emotions wrestled with one another; relieved that they would have the burden of her care but jealous that they would have the privilege of seeing to her wishes and requirements in her waning years. My transient lifestyle made it impossible for my home to be the right choice for Mom.

I experienced sadness like I had never felt when I received the call of my mother's passing. Only an intimate loss can bring about such emptiness and loneliness. I flew home on the first available flight.

Carol was tidying up some of my mother's personal effects when I entered their home. She was the picture of composure and efficiency scurrying around the house tending to the needs of those who had dropped by to convey their condolences. Her swollen red eyes were the only clue to the heartache she was experiencing while putting aside her grief to make others comfortable. We embraced, and when she handed me her handkerchief I noticed my mother's wedding

was my mother's ring really on the finger of this daughter-in-law?

set on her hand. I thought for a moment tears had clouded my vision. Was my mother's ring really on the finger of this daughter-in-law? My mother must have known as the only living female blood relative, that ring was rightfully mine.

"Carol," I tried to sound composed, "Is that Mom's wedding ring?" Of course I knew full well it was.

"Yes," Carol replied innocently, "Your mother was so sweet to leave it to me. I know how attached she was to it. Chuck would like to see me incorporate it with my own wedding band."

I felt like I was watching myself from a remote location, "Carol, she couldn't possibly have meant for you to have that ring. You must have misunderstood her intentions. I am her only daughter and you are only a part of this family through marriage. That ring belongs on my finger—not yours!"

Carol whispered, "I know how much your mother loved you. She spoke so often about how special you were to her and how proud she was of you. But, she wanted the ring to be mine for the years I cared for her."

I continued my beating, using words as my battering ram. "You took advantage of her fragility and circumstances. She had no choice but to offer you her ring. She knew you could put her out on the street at any moment. You used her and I think the courts would see it as blackmail just like you intended it to be!"

As I sat on the opposite side of the church from my only brother and his wife at our mother's funeral service, the ring on my finger felt very heavy. I wanted a "do-over". I had my mother's wedding set, but in trade I had lost my only living connection to her. God, I know it's too late, but could we discuss those punch cards now?

wake up and smell the coffee questions

☕ As we age, it is hard to remember to whom we have left possessions. Is it possible that you may have promised something to one and then later promised it to someone else?

☕ Have you created a list of things that you wish to leave certain people? Do you keep it with your will? Has it been updated?

☕ If there is an item that you know more than one person wants, have you determined to whom you would like to leave it to? Have you informed the others of your decision? If not, why?

☕ Is there a ring or some other inherited possession that you have allowed to cause a rift between you and your siblings? Is it time to forgive and forget? You taking leadership in this is powerful. Remember—your own children are watching.

peter's legacy building tips

»   Remind them with something like: "There is nothing, I repeat, NOTHING worth you fighting over when I am gone. Don't do this to your brothers and sisters (or brothers and sisters in-law), and don't do this to me. Honor me."

»   That type of communication isn't pleasant, but it might be the very thing that either helps someone grow up or at least allows others to discount their immaturity. The others might need to follow you in your bold leadership when you are gone. Show them how it is done.

»   Coach your family. Explain to them that it is normal to come to the settlement table grieving and conflicted over just what to do or say. Remind them to watch their words at such a sensitive time. They'll also need to bring a forgiving spirit if something is said that might be out of line or hurtful (intentional or unintentional).

»   Remind them that when they gather to settle your estate, that meeting will set the course of things to come for many years. Tell them to strive for a positive, generous spirit and not a "gimmie, gimmie" attitude. Will future family meetings be a joy or will they be dreaded?

ADDITIONAL THOUGHTS:
Understanding that we are human and say stupid things when we are grieving, Carol could consider approaching her sister-in-law after emotions have settled with something like, "I can see the ring means a lot to you. Please keep it. I loved your mother, and it

was an honor to care for her. Perhaps her generous affection was misplaced in giving the ring to me instead of you, but I would never take advantage of her. I feel an apology is in order."

The rift here was about more than just the ring. As with most rifts, words are spoken foolishly and cut deeply. The relationship needs healing regardless of who winds up with the ring.

7

invisible gun shot wounds

A sister and brother verbally spar for Dad's Belgium Browning 20-gauge. As told by a son who spent more than 40 years sharing the love of guns with his father.

I can't remember a time in my life when I haven't wanted to have a gun in my hands. My earliest recollections are filled with visions of guns. When I was too young to possess my own gun, I fashioned them out of anything I could. Legos, sticks, Playdoh—even my own finger could be cocked when nothing else was available. My love of guns even influenced my choice of occupation. I would become a policeman so I could carry a gun on my hip as a tool of my trade.

My memories of guns were dotted with images of my dad. I was his only son in the middle of a home filled with daughters. As a toddler I watched him clean his guns with a master's precision. As I grew older, Dad taught me the ins and outs of hunting, like passing on the rights of a sacred religion. I would follow him around field and forest, closer than his faithful mutt, filled with the hope that one day I would be mature enough to tote my own gun.

That day finally came, and we spent decades sharing every season open to avid hunters. There were pheasants in the fall along with the hallowed yearly deer hunt. Deer camp was something we only whispered about with a nod and a wink when the women-folk were around because what happens in deer camp stays in deer camp. I learned about life at my dad's side as we trudged over hill and hollow. He tried to impart to me his limited understanding of the mysteries of a woman. I witnessed a living example of his work ethic and perseverance as we tracked a wounded deer. Together we tried to understand the many injustices of life. We swapped jokes that would forever be kept between just he and I.

My dad was well into his eighties and in relatively good health when he passed away. Due to his advancing age the news was not unexpected, but the reality that he was truly gone was unbearable. Incongruent with the image of the hereafter, I found a small measure of comfort envisioning Dad enjoying a never-ending hunting day—bagging a record moose in heaven.

The larger financial matters had been handled in Dad's will, but there were some personal possessions that needed addressing. On a dismal rainy Saturday morning, the family gathered to discuss Dad's remaining belongings. Over the years, as my dad's eyesight weakened

there were some personal possessions that needed addressing

and arthritis slowed his gate, he had thinned out his hefty gun collection. Some of his less treasured models went to various sons-in-law, the vintage Remington 30.06 to his army buddy and the remaining stash left to my sisters and me to dole out. My dad had hung onto his prized Belgium Browning 20 gauge. Even in the waning years he tried to make an annual trip to keep the firing action limber along with his trigger finger. I foolishly assumed, being his son, that I would be the logical and only choice for the Browning.

When my oldest sister made the case that her son, the oldest grandson, should be given the cherished shotgun I thought she was kidding. She must be trying to interject some humor into the gloomy task at hand, but looking at her expression I realized she was deadly serious. I tried unsuccessfully to keep my composure, "Are you serious? I hunted with Dad and that gun for over 40 years. I am the next generation in line; that gun rightfully belongs to me. Not to mention the fact that Trevor never graced us with his presence on a single hunting outing. He didn't even play with toy guns as a kid, and he makes pottery in his free time!" I was either completely losing it or just plain getting sick. My dad would not have been proud, but I was fighting for his legacy-our tradition-an institution.

My sister, still stinging from my jab at her son, shot back, "You always had Dad to yourself; all his time, attention and energy. I think he owes it to me to give his oldest grandson that stupid rifle. You must have 50 guns of your own anyway. Why is one more so important?"

My head was about to explode. "Rifle? You call it a rifle? You can't even refer to it correctly—it's a shotgun! It has no place in your family. To you, hunting is finding the perfect dress on clearance. Dad would spin in his grave over this. I am not leaving these premises without that gun!" I was breathing so hard I thought I had sucked all the air from the room.

My sister confidently snapped back, "It must not have been as important to Dad as you claim or he would have spelled out his wishes for the gun in his will. The rifle, excuse me shotgun, goes to Trevor and that's the end of the matter. And by the way, shopping for things on sale is a great way to make your money go farther. You're just too stupid and lazy to look for deals! That's why you're always broke. You're right. Dad would be spinning in his grave especially if he could see the way that you blow your money."

I'm not certain what happened next. Someone called the police because I was either pushing people or throwing things, I really can't remember. But I do remember being escorted out of my childhood home by one of my fellow officers. I was so embarrassed

my sister eventually dropped the charges

when I realized what was happening, but at least he allowed me my dignity and didn't insist that I be cuffed or ride in the back of the squad car. My sister eventually dropped the charges, but not before I squirmed a bit and suffered humiliation before my colleagues.

Trevor is in possession of the beloved Browning. I fear that he's just added it to a collage of junk or sold it at a trendy art fair. I can just picture it sitting there, mangled and unappreciated.

Time has taken the edge off both the loss of Dad and the Browning; however, tragically, my sister and I have drifted further and further apart. We've just sort of gone our own ways. I don't think this is what Dad would have wanted for us, in fact I'm sure of it. But that's the way it is, and the way it will be. She drove the wedge between us, not me.

wake up and smell the coffee questions

☕ Do you have a will and other important legal documents (Durable Powers of Attorney, medical directives, etc.)?

☕ How long has it been since you have updated your will?

☕ Are you confident that it will accomplish what you wish?

☕ If you have a will, who is your executor (the person who will settle your estate according to the provisions of your will)?

- Have you chosen that person wisely?

- Does he/she understand the magnitude of what they will be asked to do? It's not just dealing with their siblings. He/she will be responsible for completing a myriad of paperwork (sale of your home or properties, distribution of your investments, dealing with an attorney, etc.).

- Is this person aware of their siblings' desires for certain items not listed in your will (a rifle or shotgun, a plate, a wedding ring, etc.)?

☕ There is no way to put a sticker on everything you own, nor should you. However, a bit of role playing could go a long way after you are gone. Something like, "Let's play, 'you wanted it, you didn't get it.' Let's say there is an item that you identify with, and after I am gone you'd really love to keep for the rest of your days. Say that item goes to someone who you think can't appreciate its value (monetary, sentimentally speaking or otherwise). What will you do? What do you think I would want you to do?"

peter's legacy building tips

» If you sense potential issues over some material possession, look 'em in the eye and instruct them with something like the following: "Get over it. Look past it. Don't dishonor me and my legacy by letting a wedge form over some 'thing.' It simply isn't worth it. Am I clear? Love your brother and sister no matter what." Get them to hear you. It may or may not help. Conflicts will inevitably arise, but you will have done the right thing. People will allow important relationships to drift. Who knows, maybe your words will come back to haunt them into growing up or guilt them a bit. No matter, they will know where you stand. So stand!

» When your children go into attack mode, it's so easy to say hurtful things that only serve to heighten the conflict. Talk to your kids about honoring you by watching their tongues. Coach them to look past the conflict even if the other party started it.

ADDITIONAL THOUGHTS:
Regarding the shotgun argument, the oldest sister—perhaps seeing how important the gun was to her brother—could have found another personal item of her father's to give her son rather than pushing her own way.

The son could have brought up the importance of the shotgun without slamming his nephew. (Stupid move.) He could have suggested choosing another item for his nephew to inherit.

sadder than death

Believe it or not, the following is based on a true story! Credit the following perspective to one anonymous funeral director.

When you've been a funeral director for 35 years you've got stories. Boy, do I have stories; tales of incredible heartbreak, funny moments wrapped in sorrow, and the down right bizarre. My job is to do all that is within my power to help families navigate unfamiliar waters and to bring them a measure of comfort.

I still chuckle when I think of an incident at the national cemetery. There was an intimate group gathered around the casket of the family's patriarch. As the color guard began their 21 gun salute a man in the crowd fainted flat to the ground. With shock and amazement a little boy said under his breath, "They shot the son of a gun!" It brought some levity to the somber assembly, if even only temporarily.

Even with a storehouse of anecdotes under my belt, I was still not prepared for the Anderson sisters. At their request, I met them at their mother's home the morning of her death. I should have walked right back out the door after our first meeting. Some situations just aren't worth any amount of money.

Emma and Rachel were in their mid sixties. They spent their life's work in education during an era when, more often than not, teachers didn't marry. Even after retirement, they remained spinsters. Rachel lived with her mother in the only house she ever owned. Emma lived a block south in a tidy modest senior complex. They were fiercely devoted to their mother and even fiercer in their competition for her affection.

they were fiercely devoted to their mother and even fiercer in their competition for her affection

I walked into the cramped dining area and joined them at the formal table. They were buried up to their elbows in little piles of bits and pieces. The table was littered with items split into two piles: two piles of necklaces, two piles of safety pins, two piles of paper clips, rubber bands, forks, spoons, knives—even individual tissues were being split. Rachel was in the process of dividing a bottle of aspirin, one tablet at a time! Emma shared sheepishly that they had begun to divide their mother's earring sets; "one silver hoop for you, one silver hoop for me" when they recognized the fallacy of that idea.

Trying to plan a service was an insurmountable challenge. Emma knew as sure as she was born that her mother's favorite hymn was "Amazing Grace," and Rachel was right as rain that it was "How Great Thou Art". My suggestion that both songs had a place in the service fell on deaf ears. Rachel insisted that her mother's favorite flower was lily of the valley and should take its rightful place in the casket spray. Emma would hear of nothing but tulips. Again I prompted, in a spirit of compromise, that the flowers would be a lovely complement to each other in the same arrangement. They completely decimated their mother's closet in the process of choosing her burial attire.

I thought we were almost finished, and I could make it home before the evening's news report, when the pendant came to their attention. Their father had bought the necklace for their mother during an overseas naval assignment shortly after they were married. There was nothing particularly outstanding about the necklace; it was just a diminutive gold chain with a small oval locket inscribed with his initials. Neither Rachel nor Emma could remember a time when it wasn't around their mother's slender neck. She had been given other jewelry as gifts over the years, but the locket held a measure of commitment and security for her. The girls agreed quickly that the locket should not be buried with their mother. Okay, so I could at least catch the later edition of the news.

Much to my amazement and with little deliberation, Emma graciously offered her rights to the necklace, stating that Rachel had carried the burden of their mother's care, and therefore, she deserved it. Maybe it was the late hour, maybe it was the emotion of the day, but I perceived Emma's generosity as a very courageous attempt at peace-making with her only living relative.

The service was lovely and went off with little fanfare. We were almost home free. The crowd had dispersed from the cemetery. The grounds-keeper began to cover the casket. I was gathering some of the funeral home's belongings when I caught a flurry of activity out of the corner of my eye. I watched in amazement as Emma, in one fluid movement, lunged forward, yanked the necklace from Rachel's throat and tossed it to the bottom of the grave. With the tenacity that would have made any NFL defensive coach proud, Rachel brought Emma to the ground with a thud and they tossed to and fro on the grass.

Rachel brought Emma to the ground with a thud

I don't know what happened after that exactly; whether or not they retrieved the necklace is a mystery. As I walked back to the hearse to return it to the garage, I thought to myself, "Yep, I truly have seen it ALL."

wake up and smell the coffee questions

☕ Are your adult children still vying for your attention in an unhealthy, dysfunctional manner? Have you considered family counseling? This type of stuff may be fodder for comedy, but it's sad. People have to grow up. Whatever you do now to help your child become more independent will serve to better prepare them for life.

☕ Do you enable this type of dysfunctional behavior?

☕ Are there some material possessions that could cause conflict among your children?

peter's legacy building tips

» Perhaps you are saying to yourself, "I'm sure my kids will fight." If you have determined that another world war is inevitable with your kids when you die, maybe you could leave all or a major portion of your estate to charity, and let them be angry at you. Please tell them you are doing it and why. This may help them grow up.

» Maybe the fight will be legitimate and justifiable. Maybe it isn't a matter of dysfunction but rather a matter of your lack of leadership. Remember, things don't have to always be equal in the way you leave your possessions. They should be "fair" but not necessarily equal. You should define the word FAIR in your world so your children don't have to. They will usually not define "fair" in the same way.

9

one man's treasure, another man's trash

This story supports the old adage above. Read how a loving granddaughter is blessed with the return of a very simple possession that was a gift from her Grandma.

I could almost smell the warm ginger cookies and potato soup as I made the long drive to my grandmother's birth home and final resting place. She was 95, so I expected the news of her passing to come any day. But when the call came, it left me feeling empty.

When I was young, my grandmother's house was like my second home. I was the first grandchild with the added bonus of being a girl. My grandma and I were exclusive members of our own mutual admiration society. I spent hours at a little handmade desk that my great-grandfather built for Grandma when she was only three. I made entire villages of people out of her empty thread spools and scraps of fabric. She taught me how to knit, although I never accomplished any of the spectacular garments she fashioned. My needles just produced long rectangular "blankets" for my dolls. She taught me how to iron Grandpa's work uniforms. We would spritz the all-cotton shirts with water and put them in the freezer for a spell. I still bear the scar on the inside of my forearm from that old relic of a steam iron.

My favorite memory was of a rather peculiar little doll Grandma bought me when I had my tonsils out. She wanted me to leave the doll at her house so I wouldn't grow weary of it like kids often do. Upon arrival at Grandma's house, I would run to the spare bedroom to check the status of Baby Muggins. Her rightful place was on the headboard of the bed I slept in during my visits. Baby Muggins had crazy stick-up hair, the color of a red crayon. She had a sweet sprinkling of freckles over her button nose. Grandma said the freckles reminded her of me. She wore a red dress with black polka dots. Grandma tucked me in each night with a prayer and a call to Baby Muggins to keep me safe and tight. I never knew what tight meant, but I knew it was something good. I always felt secure in that little bed with Baby Muggins at my side.

Years passed and I moved to various far away places but Grandma was always near and dear to my heart. Random memories of her would pop into my mind and bring a lift to my day. Fortunately, we were never more than a loving letter apart. Even when her eyes began to fail and her fingers became stiff, she still wrote to me.

fortunately, we were never more than a loving letter apart

As I reached the doorway of the small rambler of my childhood, I was reminded of the chaos of activity created when all five siblings assembled at one location. They were in a furor of commotion as they tidied up and organized Grandma's decades of belongings. I marveled at the laughter that brought everyone to tears and the pain that could actually coax a smile.

Alone in my thoughts, I walked through each cluttered room. The picture over the davenport (that's what she called a sofa) looked so small now. In my childhood, it seemed massive. Did it shrink over the years with age? I touched the handmade quilts on each bed. What was I searching for? I looked at the twin bed of my youth; Baby Muggins was not on her usual perch.

I headed into the kitchen where everyone had gathered to share a glass of Grandma's favorite sun tea. I pulled up the antique stool that had been in the same corner longer than I had been on the planet. "Has anyone seen that doll that was always perched on the shelf of the headboard in the guest room?" I looked around the room and thought maybe I had asked that question silently. I repeated more urgently, "Has anyone seen that crazy red haired doll in the guest room?" Everyone stared at me vacantly. There wasn't a hint of recognition.

Then Mary, my oldest sister, callously replied, "Oh that ugly thing? I cleared out all that junk from the guest room yesterday. That dreadful doll could frighten a child into therapy. And who in their right mind puts a red dress on a redhead? My goodness." In response to the look of horror on my face she continued, "Get over it, Jen. It's just a stupid plastic doll. Grow up!"

it's just a stupid plastic doll

My mouth went dry, and time slowed to a stop. I ran to the back porch and frantically rummaged through the garbage bags filled with plastic-canvas refrigerator magnets and doll-shaped air freshener covers lovingly knitted from scraps of yarn. There she was, hopelessly tossed aside with yesterday's Chinese take-out boxes. Her head was bent at an awkward angle, and her beautiful red hair was matted with soy sauce. I took her out of the garbage and tried to wipe her whole again with my shirt sleeve. Walking to my car with Baby Muggins, I cradled her broken head in the crook of my arm. My grandma was gone. Though I took some abuse from my sisters about the doll, having that silly doll back restored the tranquility I felt at Grandma's, regardless of their criticisms.

Years have passed since Grandma died and having Baby Muggins with me often triggers vivid memories of that special time in my life with Grandma. I now share the same warmth with my granddaughter when she visits. I tuck her in with a prayer and a call to Baby Muggins to keep her safe and tight. The other day she asked, "Grandma, what does tight mean?"

wake up and smell the coffee questions

☕ Think back. Are there any items, toys, blankets, pillows, etc. that once upon a time, a child played with incessantly?

☕ Perhaps there is some "junk" that came back from a particularly memorable trip or family event that you are about to put in the de-clutter pile to go out with the trash. Are you sure that none of that "junk" might be particularly meaningful to the people in your life who were a part of that experience? Remember, one heir's trash is another heir's treasure.

☕ Have you talked to your children or grandchildren about their interest in your possessions?

☕ Do you have this written down somewhere?

peter's legacy building tips

» Have your loved ones make a list of several things they might value of yours, and be sure they are aware of some of the seemingly worthless things you are about to place in the trash. You might be surprised at what they want to keep. Give it to them now so it doesn't become a Baby Muggins, covered in soy sauce in the local landfill. One heir could enjoy an absolute treasure.

» Maybe your heirs are not aware of what might be a treasure to them. Perhaps you might say to some, "I have that (Baby Muggins), and I need to pair down my belongings. I would like you to have it as a reminder of me." Even if they don't want it now, maybe some day they will cherish it. If they take it and wind up tossing it, it will fill their garbage can instead of yours. More importantly, you will have attempted to do something kind that many of us don't think enough of until it's too late.

» Have a garage sale, and make sure the family knows about it. You might wind up hearing, "You aren't getting rid of Baby Muggins, are you?"

10

401k not okay

The picture above illustrates this next story beautifully. Listen to one brother describe how his two "live for the moment" brothers dishonored their mother's legacy by squandering their inheritance.

Mom always saved diligently into her company retirement plan. She taught me the principles of consistent saving, paycheck after paycheck. For some reason, what she did and the way she lived was something I admired and longed to emulate. However, my two brothers, Phil and Tom, were much more "live for the moment" types, so much so that Mom wouldn't confide in them about her financial picture as she did with me. She tried to help them develop better money habits, but when she made gifts intended for them to invest for their future they would buy snowmobiles or put a down payment on a new car they really couldn't afford. (More than once, they each have had cars repossessed by the bank.)

When Mom retired, she had saved so much that she never got around to taking money out of her former employer's retirement plan except for the few Required Minimum Distributions she had to take once she turned 70 ½. I was with her when she rolled the 401k over to an IRA at a financial advisor's office. He was a good guy—honest and all that—although his New Jersey accent was a bit annoying. He did guide Mom to some investments that over the long term worked out pretty well for her.

The planner explained to us how my brothers and I could take the inherited IRA some day and continue to allow the bulk of it to grow by just taking out a little bit each year to satisfy the IRS. Mom loved the concept, but didn't want the boys to hear of it because she feared they would just blow it, especially when they heard how much she had. She kept hoping they would eventually grow a work and saving ethic. The boys knew she had money, but they had no idea how much. After all, Mom still lived in the small two and a half bedroom house that we all grew up in. In fact, her twelve year old car still looked new. She didn't care to drive much, but when I would complain to her about getting a new one she would say, "Honey, the car hasn't let me down. It gets me from point A to point B. Who do I need to impress with a car anyway?" That's the mentality that no doubt inevitably caused her to quietly become a millionaire.

At 75, Mom was the picture of health, and that's why the call that came from her neighbor about her sudden passing was such a shock. She was mowing the lawn and just fell over. That was it; a massive heart attack.

Several weeks passed and the boys and I went to see the financial advisor with the irritating Jersey accent. He disclosed the amounts that we would be receiving. The money Mom had in other non-IRA investments will get what he called a "step up" in basis. But the IRA, now worth $600,000 needed special attention for us to avoid paying lots and lots of taxes all at once.

The boys were surprisingly irritated to learn of the amount of money that Mom was leaving them. "She made us eat macaroni and gave us $50 at Christmas! What a cheapskate she was!" said Phil.

the boys were surprisingly irritated to learn of the money

I embarrassingly blurted out at them, "Shut up! Don't you have an ounce of appreciation for what she has given you?"

"Don't tell me to shut up," Phil said. "You're as cheap as she was! You can save your inheritance, but I'm going to finally get the things I deserve, and enjoy them now before I wind up next to Mom at the cemetery."

The advisor was notably aggravated with the attitude the boys demonstrated. He genuinely enjoyed serving Mom all these years. I could tell he was horrified to hear their words. He reminded us to talk to our respective income tax preparers before we left so we didn't incur unnecessary taxes at tax time.

Fast forward to April 14th of the next spring. My brother, Phil, was at his tax guy's office. He actually called me to ask if I could loan him $78,000. I exclaimed, "Are you insane? Why on earth would I consider lending money to you? Remember, I am a cheapskate, like Mom."

He pleaded, "You don't understand. I didn't withhold anything on that stupid IRA Mom left me. Combined with my regular taxes, I owe $78,000."

"You mean you spent not only the $200,000 IRA, but the other money Mom left you, too? You are kidding me, right? You were warned by Mom's financial guy not to do that."

"My buddies told me that he was all wet, and I didn't have to pay taxes on money that I inherit."

"Well, your drinking buddies were wrong. Consider the source of that wise counsel. No doubt you all drink, but at the fount of wisdom? Unfortunately NOT!"

"But I am going into foreclosure on the house I bought. I took out a mortgage, and I don't have enough equity in the house to pay this tax bill. Besides that, they came and took my new truck right off the driveway. You have to help me. What would Mom have wanted?"

"Mom always wanted you to grow up. Now it's time. You can stay in our spare bedroom for a few weeks when they throw you out of your stupid house that you never should have bought in the first place. What were you thinking? I'm not lending you a dime."

"You are as tight as Mom was. You've probably hoarded every dime you received from Mom, and feed your kids macaroni, too, no doubt! Tightwad!"

"You know something? At least I feed my kids. How long has it been since you've even seen all of your kids? You wouldn't be in such bad financial shape if you weren't paying child support to multiple women. The way you're going, you'll be paying child support until the day you die!"

CLICK!

Phil slammed down the phone, and that was the last I heard from him. My other brother didn't spend all of the IRA. (He only spent $100,000 of it. To pay the $39,000 tax bill, he took out an interest-only home equity loan. He'll wind up paying interest on it for decades to come.)

My brothers are in their 40's, but they continue to act like kids financially speaking. They've gone through what Mom left them and still aren't saving for their own retirement years. They will never grow up, and unlike Mom, I am not going to "help" them out. It would be the equivalent of flushing my money down the toilet. I came down hard on my flaky brother, but he deserved it and then some. Mom should have given it to him with both barrels like I did. I wonder if Mom would have saved as much out of each paycheck in her 401k over the years if she would have known that it was going to be flushed away after she died.

my brothers are in their 40's but they continue to act like kids

wake up and smell the coffee questions

- Have you noticed big differences between the way you and your children handle money?

- Financially speaking, do your children need to grow up? If so, what have you done to try to help them do that?

- Do you fully understand how valuable your retirement plan could be for your children if they stretch deferral over the balance of their lives?

- Have you communicated the concept of "Stretching the Inherited IRA" to your children?

- Are you certain they not only understand the complexities, but also the strategies to effectively handle inheriting your retirement accounts?

- Are you burdening one child with secrets regarding your estate?

peter's legacy building tips

The average inheritance is spent in just 17 months.

» It is especially ugly at tax time regarding these dollars in
401k's and IRA's that have never been taxed. High octane tax
for the uninformed spender. The inheritance from this type
of account moves quickly from being a blessing to a curse.

» 401k Still Okay: Meet with your advisor to talk about how
your IRA will transfer at death. You don't have to disclose
dollar amounts, but you can talk concept so they know what
to do and what NOT to do. Make sure your advisor knows
the ins and outs of "stretching" the inherited IRA and can
readily communicate this concept to your heirs.

» Give them not only the "how to handle an IRA" discussion,
but also cast a vision for what you'd like to have that
money utilized for (i.e., education of grandkids, paying off
mortgages, preparing for their own retirement years, etc.).

» Get written verification of the beneficiaries you have
selected, and make sure they are the ones you want on the
accounts. Remember, these are non-probate assets, so your
will may not direct who inherits these monies.

» If you are in a second marriage, make certain that your
beneficiary is your current spouse and not your former
spouse. If your spouses never cared for each other while you

were alive, just wait until your retirement plan winds up in the hands of your ex? OUCH!

» For the unrepentant spendthrift that you love dearly but know are never going to change, here are several considerations:

- You can establish a designated payout schedule in a number of ways that would spread out the inheritance over time.

- Help them become fiscally responsible. Coach them or challenge them to give you a monthly budget and hold them accountable to it.

- A newsletter filled with valuable financial information that goes "beyond the money" is available through our website: www. 401klatte.com. These tools could go a long way to changing your family's financial legacy.

- You could consider leaving most or all of your wealth to a charitable cause that you believe in. Why waste what you saved and potentially run the risk of doing serious harm to your spendthrift child? Tough love is true love.

hey, i'm not dead yet!

A father is forgotten and dishonored by the betrayal of a son. From the father's perspective, read this story and place yourself in his shoes.

Saturday morning the phone rang. As usual, it was my oldest son, Dave, checking in with me. He seemed to be doing fine, and I was happy to hear he got the promotion he was hoping for. I told him I was proud of him, and his mother would have been too.

He's been calling weekly since we lost his mom five years ago to cancer. I know he worries if I'll follow the strict regime of medications my doctor has me on. I don't take them as faithfully as I should, but who can keep track of all that stuff? I assured him I had already taken my morning round of pills. The drug companies won't be out of business any time soon, as long as I'm around. He let me know he'd be over to pick me up for grocery shopping around 1:00 p.m. when the grandkids were done with their karate classes.

We hung up, and I went out to get the newspaper to see what was new in the world, and that is the last thing I remember...

I woke up with machines beeping and strangers talking in medical terms I didn't understand. A man approached me and called out my name loudly, "Fred, Fred can you hear me?" I wanted to tell him that I wasn't deaf—that I indeed could hear him—but my tongue wouldn't move. I began to realize that one whole side of my body wasn't responding to anything I wanted it to do; I must have had a stroke. The neighbors saw me fall on the driveway and called 911 when I didn't respond.

> **I began to realize that one whole side of my body wasn't responding**

I managed to mumble, "AHH caaan earrr you" just as both of my boys came into the hospital room.

"Dad, don't worry about anything, the doctors are taking good care of you. They've told us they don't know exactly how long it will take for you to recover," said Paul, my youngest. The news seemed odd to be coming from him. I hadn't seen him in months, since the last time I co-signed on a new truck for him. I had been making the payments since he had some other bills that he said he needed to take care of.

Ten months to the day of the stroke Dave drove me home from the nursing home I recovered in. As we came in the back door something seemed very wrong. Many pieces of furniture along with a few of my personal possessions were gone.

"Dave, what's going on?"

"Dad, I had no idea Paul had this in mind when he promised me he'd take care of the place while you were away. He lost his job while you were in the nursing home and stayed here to save money," Dave said nervously.

My heart sank. "Dave, please sit down at my computer and log on to my local bank," I pleaded.

"Why, Dad?" he asked.

"Please, just do it!" I responded. After my wife died I added the boys to my accounts as joint tenants. My heart sank further as I looked at the zero account balances where just several months ago there had been over $185,000 in CD's, checking and savings accounts.

"I don't believe that creep!" screamed Dave.

"Quick, get him on the phone!" I retorted.

Paul answered, "Hi, Dad. How are things in the nursing home today?"

"I'm out, and I'm just about ready to kill you. Why have you done this to me?" I yelled.

why have you done this to me?

"Dad, if you are referring to the house, I was just de-cluttering it for you so it would be easy to sell," he said calmly.

"I haven't made that decision yet, Paul. We'll deal with the furniture and whatever else of mine you sold later. Where is the money in the bank accounts?" I questioned.

"Dad, I know it doesn't look good, but I have great news for you. I have gotten into the real-estate business, and I am in the process of flipping three houses I've fixed up. When they sell, the money will be back in the bank with no less than a 10% profit for the time that I have borrowed it," he explained.

"You take all of my liquid cash without telling me and offer me some 'profit'? Wasn't it enough that I've paid for your cars and most of your house payments?"

"Dad, to be honest I didn't think that you were going to make it, and that you'd be dead by now. I was only maximizing what I will inherit someday by getting a head start on growing those assets rather than letting them collect a paltry amount of interest in the bank."

"Paul, I can't even begin to put into words how much I resent the things you do and the way you live. You get my money back now! I don't care how much you have to cut the price on one of your dream homes. That money is not your inheritance! I'm not dead yet!"

that money is not your inheritance! I'm not dead yet!

"Dad, I gotta come clean. The houses aren't selling because of the real estate market slow down. People can't get the loans they need these days to buy houses. Since I fixed the houses up and ran out of money, I haven't been able to make the mortgage payments and two of the properties are already in foreclosure. I will likely lose the third one next week. They repossessed my truck last week, too. I just wanted to do something that would make you proud of me, not make you so mad at me," Paul confessed.

"Paul, I'm not mad. I'm furious. You think you are the center of the universe. Well the universe doesn't revolve around you or your get rich quick schemes!" I erupted.

"What's that, Dad? My cell phone is breaking up. I'll call you later," Paul abruptly hung up.

"That snake in the grass! He said his phone was breaking up. I'll break him up!" I bellowed, thinking this can't be good for my already fragile health.

Dave stood there stunned. "Dad, I'm so sorry. Had I known he was up to this I would have done something."

"Dave, it's not your fault. You couldn't possibly have known that your brother would have stooped to this level," I said heartbroken.

"I hope you will finally call the police, Dad. This isn't the first time that he has stolen from you. He'll do it again if he gets the chance," Dave suggested.

"Dave, I know he's a disaster, but he's still family. He's your brother. I don't want him to have a police record."

"Dad, he should be in jail for what he has done to you, and I no longer consider him my brother. He's a crook! How can you not press charges? Stop protecting him, Dad. Mom would never have let him get away with this!"

"You keep your mother out of this!"

"Dad, I was only…"

"Keep her out of it," I shouted.

Dave bit his tongue, turned and left. "Call me when you'd like to talk again," he said as the back door closed with a hollow and permanent sound.

Time has managed to bring some measure of healing, but I'll never trust Paul again. If only I would have dealt more firmly with Paul's character flaws when he was a boy. I guess I thought if I just showed him enough kindness he'd make a turn for the better. Unfortunately, he still blames other people for his mistakes.

Dave keeps insisting that I press charges and take him off my IRA as a beneficiary, but I just can't do that. He's still my son. Sadly, I know my boys will never be family again whether I am alive or dead. They despise each other and won't be in the same room together for more than a few minutes. If only I could turn back time and raise Paul differently. Instead, I ignored what was right in front of my face all those years.

wake up and smell the coffee questions

- What things do you see in your children that you know in your heart will only worsen when you die?

- Can you do more than lament the mistakes that you now know you made when your children where young? Is it really too late to do SOMETHING to affect change?

- Have you been a victim of identity theft from a loved one? Are you denying that person the benefit of serious consequences that may be the very tool needed to affect true change in his or her life?

- Have you made someone a joint tenant on some important investments? Was that the right choice?

peter's legacy building tips

»   If you have been the victim of identity theft, stop enabling the criminal and report it.

»   Has there been true repentance for mistakes that were made by you or by an adult child? Is there still a family member refusing to forgive and put the past behind them? Challenge that unforgiveness especially if there has been genuine change in the person who wounded the family.

»   Joint Tenancy with Rights of Survivorship with someone other than a spouse can be very dangerous. You may want to consider the downside to this arrangement.

»   If there hasn't been a genuine change of heart, can you really blame the offended adult child for not wanting anything to do with the person who has caused you so much harm? You can only pull a rope; you can't push it. Perhaps by beginning to deliver tough love to the dysfunctional adult child, you will eventually cause an awakening on his/her heart. The offended child may have very good cause to distrust their sibling. He/she may need to see you lead your family in tough love or your ability to lead at all may become compromised. Do what's right. Don't remain passive. How has passivity worked for you thus far?

»   Pray. You're not dead yet and neither is God.

the re(probate)

A daughter recounts how probate tied up the inheritance left by her parents, while her sister's irresponsibility with money led to financial ruin.

I always got along well with my sister. Growing up on a 200 acre farm provided us with wonderful adventures that we thought would never end. When I graduated from high school, I left for college to pursue my dream of becoming a doctor. Wendy, my sister, graduated, married her high school sweetheart and enjoyed managing a local retail store. When Dad died a few years later, Mom continued to live in the house while renting out the farming part of the property. Wendy lived just five minutes away from Mom, while I was an hour and a half away, in good traffic. As a result, Wendy helped Mom more than I did, which soon began to change our relationship as sisters.

Mom had a hard time living without Dad. I'd drive home to see her on weekends, when I was able, and help her with household chores. For me to take off to help Mom required favors and sacrifice on the part of my partners in the practice. When I got there Wendy would come over. We'd stay up late talking like close sisters do, though now we only spoke about Mom's situation. Mom's eye sight was failing, and she could no longer drive. So Wendy was called upon more than ever to drive Mom around—often several times a week.

When Wendy first started to complain, I thought it was all in good fun. She would say, "I feel like a free taxi service!" She didn't voice much else; but there seemed to be an unspoken coolness between us. I believe she began to resent helping Mom so much. She confided in me that her marriage was troubled. She and her husband, David, were fighting constantly. Between still grieving for Dad, toting Mom around, and the stress of her marriage, she was not in a good place emotionally. To compensate for driving Mom around, I gave her money for gas and wear and tear on her car. I even added a little extra for her time. She always took the money saying she "deserved it."

One weekend I was slated to come up for a weekend to see Mom. Just before I left the house, the phone rang; it was my partner who would be covering for me the next few days. He was gravely ill from food poisoning. In fact, he was calling me from his hospital bed. He obviously was in no shape to cover for me, so I simply had to cancel my trip back home. I called Wendy several times; she didn't answer her home or cell phone. I regretfully left several messages.

she was livid and began to insult me in a way she never had done before

She returned my call several hours later. She was livid and began to insult me in a way she had never done before. I tried to explain my situation and apologize, but she refused to listen or accept my apology. "Just because you are a doctor doesn't mean you are better than anyone else and can do whatever you want. You don't care about Mom. All you care about is your job!" The insults continued; it was obvious Wendy was jealous of my life. I finally just hung up.

After attempting to calm down, I called Mom. She understood my situation and was much more forgiving than Wendy. She also offered some insight into my sister's irrational behavior. Things were worsening in her marriage. I served as the "straw that broke the camel's back". My anger softened and was replaced by compassion.

That was the last conversation I had with Mom. The following Monday, Wendy called and—between sobs—told me Mom had passed away in her sleep. I quickly made arrangements to reschedule my patients and hurried home to help Wendy deal with funeral arrangements. It was obvious that she was still angry with me, despite our grief. When I apologized for the umpteenth time, she calmed down, and we were able to deal with the details of the funeral.

When our conversation veered toward the discussion of our inheritance, Wendy's demeanor changed. She thought the inheritance would be the boost her marriage so desperately needed. "My realtor friend tells me this place is worth over a million dollars, and city folks are moving up here in droves! That means we both would get over $500,000!" she said excitedly. I had no idea the property was worth that much. That was about all Mom and Dad had, while their meager savings went to pay for their funerals.

Two weeks after the funeral, I drove up to see Wendy and visit with Mom and Dad's attorney. I assumed I was the executor since

I was the oldest, and Dad had told me he felt I was the more level-headed one. When the attorney said Wendy was the executor, it felt like a slap in the face. I suppose they felt that because Wendy lived closer, she should execute their wills. I focused on the logic of the situation, but it still stung. The attorney reminded us that our Mom's estate would need to pass through the probate process. He explained that probate is usually non-problematic and only gets caught up if the will is contested or an asset doesn't liquidate.

When we left the attorney's office, I couldn't help but notice that Wendy was unusually happy and in good spirits. She said, "Sis, come for a ride with me." I got in her pickup truck and she drove out to a remote section of town near the lake. She stopped and we both got out of the truck. She pointed, "See that hill there? That's where my new house will be located."

I was stunned. "Wendy, it's beautiful; but, isn't it too soon? Please tell me that you're buying this land on the contingency that your own house sells first," I was concerned.

She smiled and said, "You will always be a kill-joy that crosses every stinking 't' and dots every stinking 'i', won't you?" You're forgetting about our windfall of money?"

"No, I'm not forgetting, but neither one of us knows how long the probate process will take. What if the property doesn't sell right away?" I suggested.

"My friend says the property will sell fast. There are so many city folks buying homes here right now!"

"Wendy, they are buying vacation homes around the lake, not hundred acre farms that require tons of work! What if you don't get your inheritance right away? What about your marriage?

Wendy, please try to back out of this deal!" I pleaded desperately.

Wendy snapped back, "When I want a doctor's advice, I'll go to my clinic, thank you! Keep your nose out of this!"

TWO YEARS LATER

Well, the will was never contested, but the probate process is not finalized because the property has not sold. We spent the first eight months getting the title cleared so we could put it on the market. There were easement and domain issues to resolve regarding the future expansion of a county road running through the property. After all the red tape and bureaucracy, we finally got the green light to sell. It has been on the market for well over a year with little interest. People are buying the smaller vacation homes.

Wendy is in danger of losing her own home due to the land and construction loan payments on her new property. The financial stress proved to be too much for her marriage, and David recently filed for divorce. I helped her with loan payments, but it only served to further fuel her resentment towards me. She finally stopped returning my calls, so I am no longer informed about the probate process. I've had to hire an attorney to help me stay-in-the-loop. My sister isn't communicating with me, and frankly, I no longer trust her.

As we continue to add legal fees, we lowered the price of our property twice, and the probate process drags on. We are ultimately diminishing our own inheritance. I know it's wrong but I find myself oddly enjoying the fact that we aren't going to inherit what we were originally hoping. This is driving Wendy crazy. That's wrong. I know. I don't wish her any harm, but she has treated me so badly. Now she is getting her "just desserts." Two sisters who once enjoyed each other no longer speak. The family farm that once brought us joy and adventure, keeps us apart.

wake up and smell the coffee questions:

- Have you discussed the pros and cons of going through probate with an estate planning attorney?

- Do you fully understand which assets are most likely to go through the probate process?

- Are you aware of a "need" that any of your heirs may have to receive your inheritance quickly after you pass? If so, do you feel compelled to attempt to make a special provision for that quick disbursement?

- Do they (your heirs) understand that although probate is usually non-problematic, significant delays and expenses can arise, especially if the will is contested or if an asset takes longer to liquidate than expected?

- Are you aware of any latent resentment between your heirs that could erupt into relationship-damaging combat?

- If you are aware of possible issues, have you discussed those concerns with your estate planning attorney?

- Do you believe your attorney fully understands you and what you hope to accomplish with your legal documents?

- Do you and your heirs understand the tax implications of how your estate is structured?

peter's legacy building tips

» While fair is most definitely not always equal, you might want to discuss your decisions to favor (or extend extra help to) one heir over another with all of the parties involved. Don't assume that your over-achiever doesn't crave and need your approval. That may be a flawed assumption regardless of how successful that child is. Tell that child that you are indeed proud of him or her. That may mean more to that individual than any amount of money or material wealth you leave to them.

» Have you challenged your under-achiever to continue to grow and develop as an individual regardless of their income level? They too need to be affirmed that regardless of what they do, you care about them as well. If you have been comparing one to the other, stop now. Challenge the one under-achiever to celebrate their siblings' successes and to be genuinely happy for them. More importantly, affirm the unique abilities that you see in them. Encourage them to see it, develop it and use it.

» This book can't and won't give you legal advice. That is why it is imperative that you find a good estate planning attorney. You do need to decide for yourself as to whether or not you want to have your estate go through the probate process. Again, discuss that with an attorney whom you trust and who understands your legacy goals. Probate, as attorneys tell us, is usually uneventful, timely and relatively cheap.

» Are you feeling overwhelmed and a bit intimidated by the whole idea of estate planning? That's okay. Just know you can't possibly help your heirs avoid every possible conflict. However, your steadfast leadership may leave enough of an imprint on their lives to help them wisely deal with conflict when it arises. As the author, Max Lucado, says, "Conflict is inevitable; combat is avoidable."

» This story may leave you with the impression that probate is inherently evil. It is not. The dictionary defines probate as the official proving of a will as authentic or valid in a probate court. Its people's character (or at times lack thereof) and circumstances that may be beyond our control that can delay the probate process or make it especially costly—not the process itself. You need to be aware of what is motivating you to appoint one heir over another as executor. You need to do as good a job as you can of planning. You need to be aware of the "undercurrents" that exist among your heirs. The more informed decisions you can make regarding probate, the more you can determine to what lengths you will go in order to avoid it. Maybe avoiding it is a worthwhile goal. Then again, maybe not. You decide after you've created your vision for your legacy and after you sought competent legal counsel.

in their hands for good (not just forever, but for their good)

You can influence your family tree or legacy. A man tells the story of his bad inheritance ordeal and determines to proactively help his own children to avoid inheritance pitfalls.

I never understood what my brother, Jerry, saw in her. When he married Susan we were all a bit bewildered. She was rarely pleasant and seemed annoyed most of the time—her face had a permanent scowl. But, if she could make Jerry happy, I guess that's all that really matters.

Jerry and Susan lived about three blocks away from Mom, who still lived in the house we grew up in. When my brother Scott and I graduated from college, we both moved to Minneapolis, but occasionally visited Mom in Duluth. We were glad that Jerry lived so close to Mom, since we were a couple of hours away if she needed help. Mom was in her early eighties.

About ten years ago, Mom attended a seminar on avoiding probate. The attorney teaching the seminar encouraged the use of Revocable Living Trusts. Mom didn't see much point in getting a trust; but she was adamant about avoiding probate after she heard all the horror stories the attorney shared. (Personally, I think they were over the top.)

After some consideration, Mom decided to put the house, family cabin and her mutual funds in joint tenancy with Jerry so she would avoid probate on those assets. Scott and I didn't think much of it at the time. The three of us were listed as her primary beneficiaries on her IRA's and her annuities. When Mom died, we learned that avoiding probate on the other assets generated a whole new set of problems.

Scott and I trusted Jerry implicitly, as did Mom, of course. What none of us realized was in order for him to split those assets with us, he had to sell them first and pay a capital gains tax. (Years later, I learned from a financial planner that if the house, cabin and mutual funds had stayed in Mom's name, there would not have been capital gains taxes on them because of something called a "Step –Up in Basis".)

To make matters worse, he was limited to giving Scott and I no more than $12,000 a year or he would pay gift taxes. It literally was going to take 14 years to pay us our share of the inheritance. We received our inheritance from the IRA's and the annuities right away, but the proceeds from the other assets were tied up. I couldn't help but think that Jerry's wife, Susan, smugly enjoyed the fact that Scott and I had to wait years to get our share of Mom's estate. She never said much when we got together to discuss it, but I got a sense there was hint of glee behind that permanent scowl.

Neither of us liked the idea of having to wait so long to get what we should have had coming to us, but that is what happened. That is, until Jerry got sick with lung cancer. Sadly, he died in just a few months. Scott and I didn't know that when he sold the cabin, the house and the mutual funds, he put the money into CD's at the bank. No problem, since CD's are always safe, right? Wrong!

Without thinking through all the implications, he titled the CD's with Susan as a Joint Tenant with Rights of Survivorship. The annual gifts that had come to us for a few years stopped abruptly. We phoned Susan about this, and she just said, "I think your mom wanted Jerry to have that money. He never should have given you a dime, as far as I was concerned. We were the ones that took care of your mom in her last months. You shouldn't have received what Jerry insisted on sending you. Well, that's over, unless you are going to try to get money from a widow."

he never should have given you a dime, as far as I was concerned

Shocked, I replied, "You are out of your mind. That money is my mother's money. It's Scott's and my inheritance. Sure, you should get Jerry's piece, but you better give us ours or…"

"Or what"? Susan shot back. "You have to know that the acronym JTWROS means *Joint Tenants with Rights of Survivorship*. Jerry had the right to put money into joint tenancy with his wife. He's dead, and you want to take his widow's money? I have the right, and you have no right. Goodbye."

That was the last conversation I had with Susan. Mom sure avoided probate, but she also unknowingly disinherited two of her sons on a large part of her estate. The injustice of what she did still galls me. Over time I've let it go and focused on raising my own family. My daughters and son are now through school and have their own lives.

Recently, my wife and I met with our financial advisor. He presented us with the idea of being proactive in how our estate would be transferred to our children. He encouraged us to think hard about how our children might honor us when we are gone and how to communicate our wishes to them. We worked on the details of our estate, reviewed our will and trust documents and compiled our thoughts in a Document of Honor. He then scheduled a meeting with our children to help us present this information and to instruct them about common pitfalls, like the improper use of JTWROS, spending inheritances without thinking about the future and money management. Needless to say, he got my attention.

At first, our kids were a bit reluctant to talk about our inevitable passing. When I had one of my sons on the phone, he asked, "Dad, you aren't dying are you?"

"No, son, at least not that I am aware of. But, I'm going to die someday. Though you may not understand it at first, I am not going to run the risk of leaving you and your sisters in a mess when I'm gone. I can't guarantee you won't have a conflict or two along the way. But I'm making my intentions crystal clear so there will be no doubt about how I want you to honor your mother and I when we are gone. There's nothing we own that's worth fighting over. We want and need you to stay together, to continue to be a family and to look out for each other. That's what the meeting with our advisor is about. Sure, we'll cover some boring details of probate and taxes at death. More importantly though, we are going to do all that we possibly can to lead you and your sisters in family unity and financial common sense. We want to make sure that what we have worked so hard to accumulate will transfer over into your hands for your good. We want your inheritance to be a blessing and not a curse."

"Okay, Dad. I'll be there. No worries." He got it.

I am thankful my children won't have to go through the misery I endured when my mother and Jerry died. I am confident that my estate is set up properly, and my children have been instructed on how to "inherit well". It isn't easy to think about our children's lives after we are gone, but I know my wife and I have done everything we can to leave a legacy of more than just money—a legacy of family unity and love.

my children have been instructed on how to 'inherit well'

wake up and smell the coffee questions:

☕ Have you sought wise counsel from your attorney, accountant and/or financial planner, people who have been through the estate settling process a number of times?

☕ While probate could be a problem, are your fears causing you to overreact by possibly using joint tenancy with non-spouses, over-use of P.O.D. or T.O.D (Paid/Transfer on Death), or giving property away to heirs before you really want to, etc.?

☕ Have you thought through the implications of leaving too much in one heir's name thereby burdening that person with the distribution of your wealth? Your trust in them may not be the issue that causes you to inadvertently disinherit your family.

☕ How would you like it if your lack of good counsel ended up disinheriting those closest to you? Good advice isn't necessarily cheap, but it's far less expensive than bad advice or no advice.

peter's legacy building tips:

» While I am 100% in favor of calling family meetings, I am aware of the fact that a "call to meet" can be a bit unnerving for some of the kids, especially if it seems to come out of left field. I suggest you broach the topic thoughtfully.

» One way to approach the subject of your estate with your children is in the story. Here is another way: "We recently reviewed the various ways that assets pass to heirs in terms of what goes through probate and what does or doesn't get taxed at death. Don't be worried. Nobody is dying, but we are aware of a need to better understand how what we own may transfer someday." (Maybe add some levity.) "That is, if I don't run off to Vegas, and blow it all before I kick the bucket."

» Open up the conversation so the kids don't feel like gold diggers in order to get this stuff out in the open. There's absolutely nothing wrong with an honest, open conversation about the inevitable. Someone has to take the lead. Do it now, while you can make certain "demands" and haven't yet lost your opportunity to influence them. We only get a certain number of years before old age robs us of our former selves and the role reversal takes full effect. Speak truth into your adult children's lives now. Set the expectations and leave no room for misunderstanding of your intentions.

» Regarding Joint Tenancy with Rights of Survivorship: As a general rule, only title assets that way with a spouse. After seeing your estate planning attorney they may not want you to hold any assets that way. If you have confidence in your attorney, follow their lead if they advise against JTWROS. They've more than likely lived out the nightmares of unintended and disinherited heirs via their clients.

» Once again, while getting your legal work done is essential, it's up to you to continue to put the finishing touches on your parenting role by articulating unity, honor and a legacy that's worth remembering. The legal work can help, but it is not able to replace strong leadership. The future of your family is depending on you saying what so many tell me is already understood. Say it anyway—and at the risk of redundancy—say it often.

before your last cup of coffee

The following is a brief overview of my Legacy Building Tips found after each story.

» Whether the kids wish to face it or not, you are going to die some day. They can live in denial, but it is still denial nonetheless.

» When you are gone, they are going to come to the settlement table. There's no getting around it or away from it.

» When you are gone, their conflicting emotions may erupt into arguments, hurt feelings and disunity that in many cases never gets resolved. Past hurts and unfinished business may also make things difficult. The assumption that the kids will never fight can be oh, so wrong! Is there something that can be resolved today to make tomorrow easier?

» Don't assume that your heirs fully understand how to honor you when you are gone. Communicate what having that right spirit would look like.

» Tell them there is nothing you own worth them fighting over. Attempt to divide up your material possessions by developing a list (perhaps with their help), and put it with your will.

»   Stress the importance of family unity. Leave that legacy clearly in mind.

»   Have them meet with your financial planner to help them understand your estate.

»   Instruct them on how to inherit certain assets that can trigger tax time bombs such as IRA's, 401K's, 403(b)'s, etc.

»   After you have had conversations with your heirs, you should revisit your legal documents to be certain they are still appropriate.

»   Visit our website www.401klatte.com or call us at 952-882-0400 for assistance.

beyond cabinosity:

additional services from
The 401k Latte Company

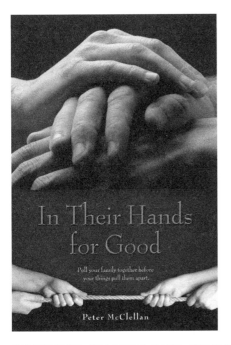

IN THEIR HANDS FOR GOOD

The average inheritance is spent in just 17 months. Worse yet, many siblings go to their grave hating each other. We have seen adult children end up speaking to each other only through their attorneys after they inherit their parents' estate.

Without proper planning and communication with heirs, many estate plans fail. Unwilling to discuss end-of-life issues, families are only leaving themselves open to conflict. The *In Their Hands for Good*sm program is meant to help families start communicating about what really matters. Through a series of conversations, parents can be proactive in preparing their children for the potentially difficult time of settling their estate.

We also discuss the emotion of money. Without some degree of coaching, it's not uncommon that heightened emotions torpedo the estate settling process. The program attempts to educate both parents and children on basic financial principles and how to "inherit well." Do the hard work today so your estate will be "In Their Hands for Good."

Because every life tells a story

Reel Legacy Conversation

REEL LEGACY CONVERSATION
Reel Legacy Conversation is a process of video and/or audio taping of an individual's life's priorities in their own words. DVD's are created with the intention of allowing family and future generations to understand you, what you stood for, and what has made you, you. Far beyond the sterile documents of a will or a trust, this service can provide a lasting, vivid testament to the value that your life has had on others, especially those you hope to influence long after you are gone. It's our conviction that every life tells a story. Visit our website at www.401klatte.com.

STAY RETIRED SOLUTION[sm]

Stay Retired Solution challenges our clients to look ahead to what they are retiring *to* not just what they are retiring *from*. There is a practical emphasis on several key questions most of us need to address financially, such as:

- Am I going to be okay?

- Am I on the right track?

- Am I in the right stuff?

- Should I continue working? Why or why not?

We help support our clients so they can stay retired. Over the years we have identified key minefields of retirement and common mistakes that can be avoided. This conversation goes beyond the money.

MUST AND OUGHTS INSTRUCTIONS

So often when people inherit retirement plans from parents and other non-spouses, they are prone to make knee-jerk reactions that cause unnecessary taxation and penalties. This instructional document is developed to provide direction after your death. It is not a legal document, but it may be beneficial to keep with your will and/or trust documents; a must for someone with tax deferred dollars.

INHERITANCE TRANSITION SUPPORT

Strong, administrative support and coordination for heirs in settling, re-titling, and distributing inherited assets after the death of a loved one. This whole process is often overwhelming for heirs. We can help provide leadership and direction to get this process moving efficiently and effectively. Currently only available in the Minneapolis/St. Paul metro area.

401k Latte Company
10543 165th Street West
Lakeville, MN 55044
952-882-0400
www.401klatte.com

a special thank you to...

My wife, Sally, whose commitment to excellence never lets me settle for the compromising comfort of mediocrity.

My children John, Dan and Julia, who love me unconditionally and create in me a desire to leave a legacy they will be proud of.

Kelly Schackman, my co-author and friend—you are destined for greatness.

My team at the 401k Latte Company: Debbie Bougie, whose faithful service to this company has helped it become what it is today. Emily Iverson, who helps keep me on task (not an easy job). Scott Jacobson, who challenges me to develop "beyond the money" services for my clients.

Caron Young, whose years of professional editing experience have benefited us greatly.

Joe Beard, whose creativity is amazing and has driven the visual impact of this book!

Kathy Grunditz, for her visual impact and laying out my manuscript into book form.

John Murphy, a friend and attorney, for his legal insight and encouragement.

author bios

PETER MCCLELLAN
Peter McClellan, President of the 401k Latte Company, has
assisted investors for more than 20 years. He has invested in
literally thousands of conversations with his financial planning
clients about their money, their families and their life goals. He
has been privileged to observe legacies being created, lived out
and passed on. He's also been grieved to witness legacies lost,
inheritances wasted and families fractured with disunity. He
prefers to optimistically believe that it's never too late to pull
families together and lead them to unity. Inheritances can be a
blessing and not a curse.

KELLY SCHACKMAN
Kelly is happily married to her prince, Tony. They have six
children and the marvelous blessing of five grandchildren. With
all the busyness of life, she still manages to pen a few lines here
and there along with lots and lots of laundry and dishes.

From her earliest memories she recalls writing tales of fairies,
horses and castles, and when she was older, a few campy romance
stories. Cabinosity is an opportunity for Kelly to realize a
childhood dream, and she is honored to have co-authored this
work with Peter. Not yet the best-selling great American novel, a
girl's gotta start somewhere.

works cited

10   *"Remember not only to say"* Franklin Templeton Investments. <u>Quotations of Benjamin Franklin</u>. Bedford, MA: Applewood Books, Inc., 2003: Page 16.

73, 101   *"The average inheritance"* Stan Hutchinson. *San Diego Daily Transcript,* March 3, 2004.

90   *"As the author Max Lucado"* Max Lucado. <u>When God Whispers Your Name</u>. Thomas Nelson Publishing, 1999: Page 44.

a personal note from peter

Perhaps you have personally connected to one or more of the short stories. You may have experienced a similar nightmare after the passing of a loved one, and the hurt is still new. I am sorry you have had a bad experience. It is my prayer, however, that this book will help you deal with the difficult issues surrounding death and the settling of an estate.

If this book has been helpful or has impacted your family, please share your story with us. You can email us at sally@401klatte.com.

May your children know what to expect, be aware of your wishes and forever **honor** your legacy.